SEA FISHES
of Southern Africa

QUESTIONS AND ANSWERS

Q A

Text: Mike Bruton
Illustrations: David Thorpe

STRUIK

Contents

Struik Publishers (Pty) Ltd
(a member of The Struik Publishing Group (Pty) Ltd)
Cornelis Struik House
80 McKenzie Street
Cape Town 8001

Reg. No.: 54/00965/07

First Published 1995

Editor Susannah Coucher
Designer Robert House
Cover designer Darren McLean
Illustrator David Thorpe

Typesetting by Deirdré Geldenhuys, Struik DTP
Reproduction by Unifoto (Pty) Ltd, Cape Town
Printed and bound by Kyodo Printing Co (Pte) Ltd, Singapore

ISBN 1 86825 682 0

Introduction

Our wildlife heritage is made up of many different kinds of birds, mammals, reptiles, amphibians, insects and other animals on land, as well as an abundance of spectacular plants and animals that live in our seas and fresh waters. Sea fishes in particular, are abundant and serve as a valuable resource if they are carefully conserved. Each one of us can play a very important role in this conservation if we are well informed about fishes. The study of fishes is called ichthyology, and the study of the use and conservation of fish stocks is called fisheries science.

Can you guess the names of these sea fishes? The answers are on page 32.

What is a fish?

Fishes are cold-blooded, backboned animals that live in water. There are three different groups: jawless fishes; sharks and rays; and bony fishes. They are as different from one another as frogs, snakes, mammals and birds. The three different groups of fishes share a way of life in water and have many different forms.

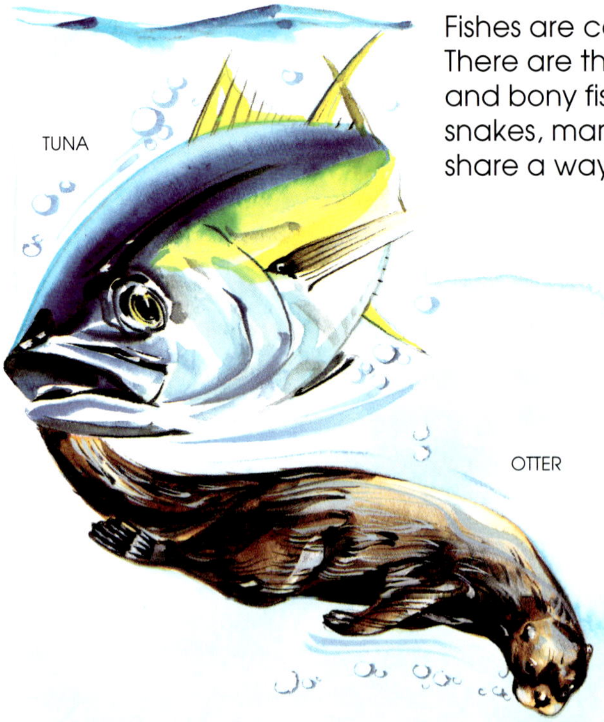

How are fishes different from marine mammals?

A fish, such as a tuna or mullet, is a cold-blooded animal which breathes through its gills, normally has scales and fins, and either lays eggs or gives birth to live young. A marine mammal, such as a seal or otter, is warm-blooded, which means that it breathes air using its lungs, has a hairy or furry skin, and always gives birth to live young.

How many fins do fishes have?

A typical fish, such as a blacktail, has seven fins – two paired fins and three unpaired fins. The pectoral and pelvic fins are paired but the dorsal, tail and anal fins are unpaired and lie along the central line of the body. Many fishes have two dorsal fins. The dorsal, tail and anal fins of eels are joined.

Why do fishes have different body shapes?

Fishes have many different body shapes so that they can swim and feed in different ways. Oval, streamlined fishes, such as tunas, are designed to swim fast and to catch their prey at high speed. Flattened fishes, like skates, hunt along the bottom and hide themselves in the sand. Eels are long and thin so that they can feed and shelter in narrow crevices. Butterflyfishes are narrow so that they can squeeze through small gaps and dart to and fro.

What are the different kinds of fins used for?

The pectoral fins of the butterflyfish are used for many different types of activities, such as hovering, swimming, turning, stopping, and fighting displays. Flyingfishes use their pectoral fins as 'wings' for gliding. The dorsal and anal fins of the kob keep the fish on a steady course, like the fins of a submarine, and the powerful tail fin pushes the fish forwards. The pelvic fins keep the fish level while swimming and they are also used for stopping. In clingfishes, the pelvic fins are joined to form a sucking organ to attach the fish to rocks.

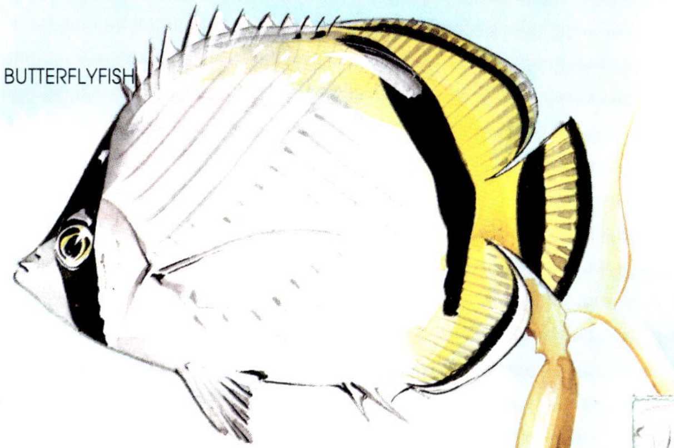

FISH SCALES

Why do fishes have scales?

The scales on a fish's body protect it from predators and parasites because it forms a flexible armour coating. The rows of scales bend with the swimming movements of the fish to make a smooth, streamlined body-shape over which the water flows smoothly. Some scales, which are found in a line along the middle of the body, have tiny pits that are used to measure the speed of water currents.

Why do tunas have warm blood?

So that they can swim quickly for a long time. In the tunas, the warm blood leaving the muscles passes through a network of capillaries which shift heat into the cold blood that is entering the muscles. In this way the swimming muscles work at the high temperatures that are needed for high-speed swimming.

Are all fishes cold-blooded?

Most fishes are cold-blooded animals. This means that their body temperature is usually low and it changes with the temperature of the water. Some large, fast-swimming fishes, such as tunas, marlins, and the mako and great white sharks, keep their body temperature above that of the water temperature.

Human embryo

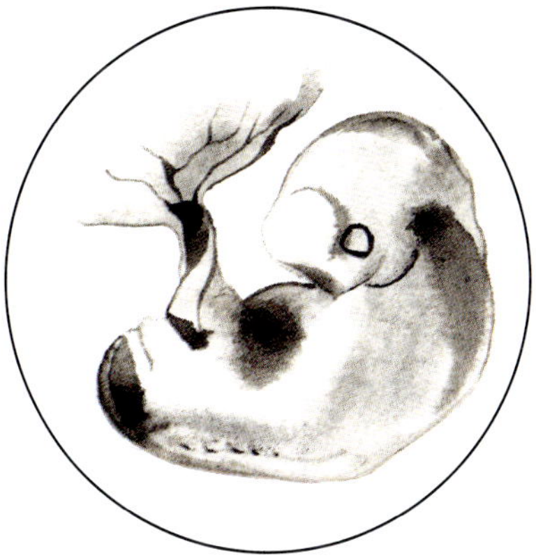

Did you know?

Unborn human babies about 28 days old look like fishes. They have simple gill openings and a tail and live in a water-filled sac inside their mother. This shows that we evolved from a fish-like animal.

FOSSIL FISH

The variety of fishes

There are many more different kinds of fishes than there are frogs, snakes and lizards, birds and mammals! Fishes first appeared in the fossil record over 100 million years before all other backboned animals, and they have always been common in seas and fresh waters. It isn't surprising that fishes are so successful as 78 per cent of the Earth's surface is covered by water. Many marine fishes live along shallow coasts but fewer species occur in deep water.

Why are there so many marine fishes?

The richness of our sea fishes is because of the incredible variety of underwater habitats which are found off the coast. These habitats range from coral reefs, rocky and sandy shores to mud flats, estuaries, lagoons, and oceans which are over 5 000 metres deep. Another reason is that South Africa is the meeting place of three great oceans – the Atlantic, Indian and Southern Oceans and has fishes from all these oceans. South Africa has more marine fish families than the Philippines or Australia, but less than Japan.

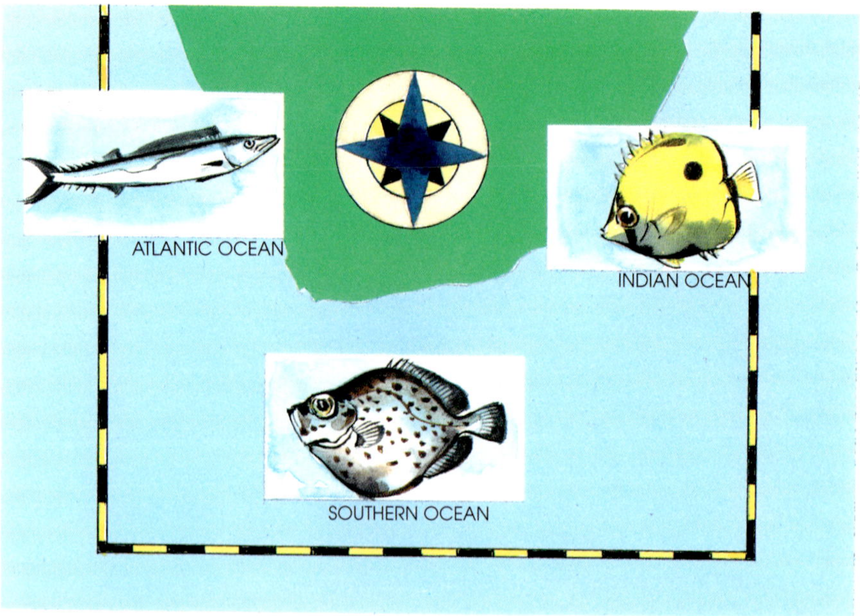

Which is the largest fish?

The plankton-eating whale shark is the largest fish. A giant, 12,65 metres long and weighing over 15 000 kilograms, was once caught off Pakistan, but they may even reach over 18 metres in length.

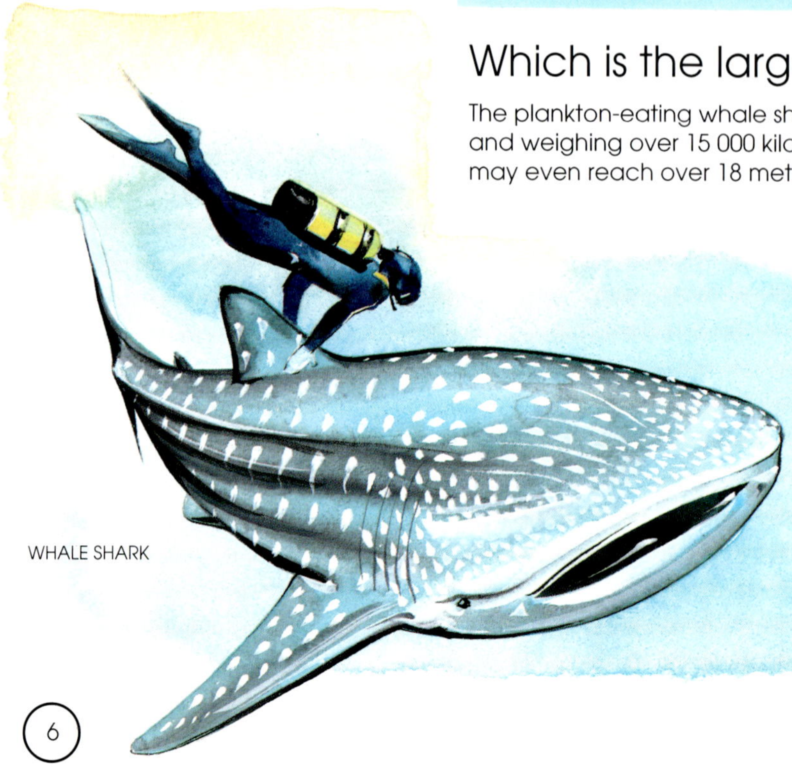
WHALE SHARK

How many fishes are there?

There are about 24 000 species of fishes in the world. Of these, about 15 000 live in the sea and 9 000 live in fresh waters and estuaries. Over 2 300 species of marine fishes live off the coast of southern Africa, which is about 9,6 per cent of the world's total fish fauna. About 150 species of fishes live in South African estuaries.

HUNTING FOR FISH

Are new species of fishes still being discovered?

Yes, several new species of fishes are discovered each year, some by anglers, children or holidaymakers. In 1979 Mark Pote, an18-year-old, found an interesting pufferfish in a tidal pool while on holiday in Port Alfred. He took the fish to the JLB Smith Institute of Ichthyology in Grahamstown. The scientists there found that it was a new species of fish, and so they named the fish after him.

Which is the fastest fish in southern Africa?

The sailfish, which can swim at speeds greater than 109 kilometres per hour over a short distance. This is faster than a cheetah, the fastest mammal, which can reach 96 kilometres per hour. Other fast fishes include the marlin, the wahoo, and the yellowfin tuna, as well as the swordfish and some of the larger sharks. A speeding tuna can move its tail at an amazing 10 beats per second!

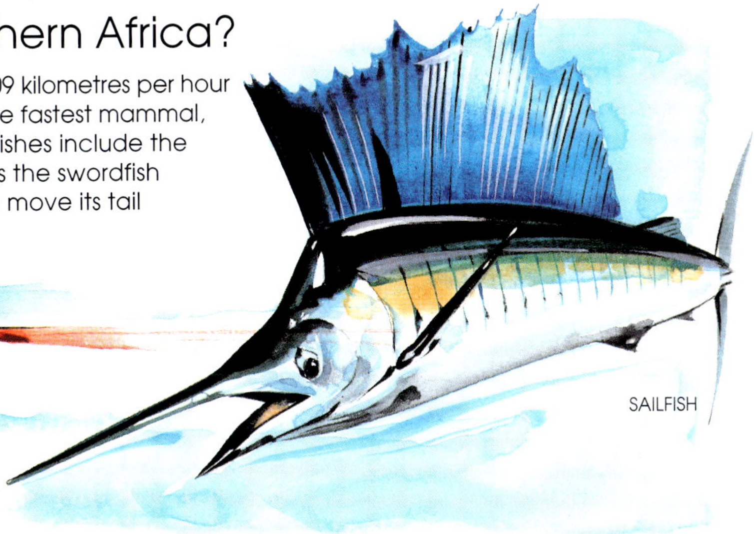

SAILFISH

DWARF GOBY

Which is the smallest fish?

Gobies are the smallest fishes and the shortest backboned animals. The smallest fish in the world is a dwarf goby from Chagos archipelago which is only 8,6 millimetres long in males and 8,9 millimetres long in females. The smallest fish in southern Africa is another dwarf goby that reaches 16 millimetres in length.

Do any marine fish live only in South African waters?

Yes, at least 280 species of marine fishes in southern Africa are not found anywhere else. These indigenous fishes are mainly klipfishes, gobies, seabreams, catsharks and toadfishes. The carpenter, Fransmadam, dageraad, red stumpnose, janbruin, musselcracker and red steenbras are examples of indigenous seabreams.

RED STUMPNOSE

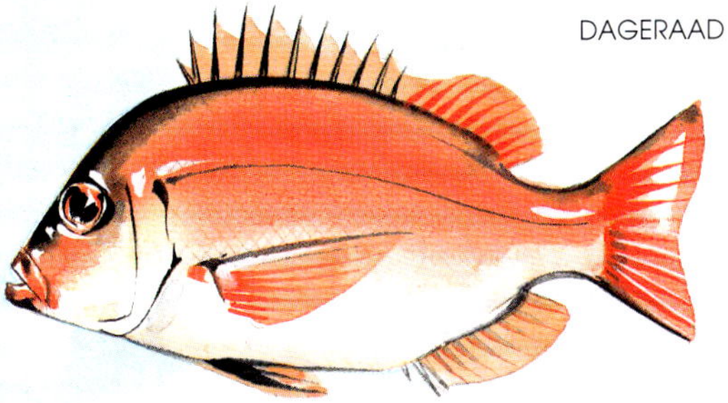

DAGERAAD

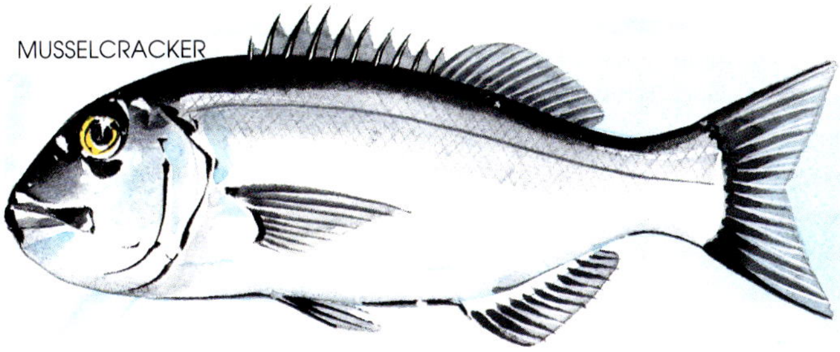

MUSSELCRACKER

Sharks and their cousins

Sharks, rays and chimaeras have skeletons made of cartilage. They are the lions and eagles of the sea because they feed on other sea creatures. Cartilaginous fishes can move as quickly in the water as birds do in the air, and may swim across wide stretches of ocean. They have large brains and a good sense of sight and taste. They can also detect underwater vibrations using special sense organs.

Are sharks really primitive?

No. Although the basic shapes of sharks have changed very little for millions of years, they have developed brains, skeletons, teeth and fins that are as advanced as those of the bony fishes. Among the most advanced of all fishes are the devil-rays which are birdlike and have rather large brains.

LIFE CYCLES OF SHARKS AND RAYS

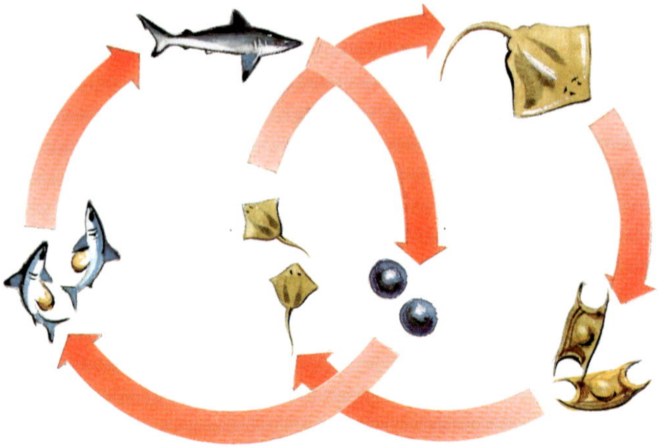

How many sharks are there?

There are about 1 110 species of cartilaginous fishes in the world's oceans. Of these, about 470 species are sharks, 570 are skates and rays and 70 are chimaeras, ratfishes and elephantfishes. In southern Africa there are about 110 species of sharks, 64 skates and rays and 8 chimaeras, which is a total of 182 species of cartilaginous fishes. Sharks are even more common in Australia.

How do sharks and rays breed?

They either lay their eggs in hard cases which protect them from hungry predators or give birth to live young which can swim into hiding places. Unlike most bony fishes, sharks and rays produce only a few eggs or young – usually less than 50 each year. The young are released at birth and are not guarded by their parents. The eggs in the egg cases hatch after two to twelve months.

SHARK CAGE

Do sharks attack people?

A very small number of sharks attack people, probably because they mistake them for their natural prey. No shark will eat people as a normal part of its diet. Not many sharks found off South Africa are dangerous to humans. Of these, the three most dangerous are the great white, the Zambezi and the tiger shark. These are the same sharks that are dangerous off Australia. In KwaZulu-Natal, anti-shark nets protect swimmers from sharks.

Which is the largest shark ever?

The extinct great-tooth shark, which reached a length of 17,8 metres. This is about three times the length of a car! The largest predatory shark found in South African waters is the great white shark which reaches 7,9 metres and 3 500 kilograms. The smallest shark in South Africa is the 20-centimetre-long dwarf shark.

DWARF SHARK

Do sharks have to swim all the time to breathe?

No. Some sharks can pump water over their gills by opening and closing their mouth cavity while they are not swimming. Most of the large, fast-swimming sharks do have to keep moving so that they can take up enough oxygen from the water passing over their gills.

DEEPSEA COELACANTHS

The amazing coelacanth

Over 120 species of extinct coelacanths are known from fossils, which are remains of animals preserved in rocks. We have learnt from these fossils that coelacanths are an ancient group of fishes which are about 400 million years old. Amphibians, reptiles, birds and mammals on land may have evolved from a relative of the coelacanth. The fossil record of this fish stopped abruptly about 65 million years ago and they were thought to have disappeared forever. It was a great surprise when a living coelacanth was caught near East London in South Africa in 1938.

How many coelacanths are there?

There may be less than 1 000 coelacanths worldwide. The German diver and scientist, Hans Fricke, counted coelacanths off the coast of Grand Comoro using a submarine designed for research and found that there are about 500 adults there. A smaller number occurs off Anjouan island. Coelacanths probably also live on the East African coast, but we are not sure how many there are.

What do coelacanths eat?

Fishes, such as reef fishes, snipe eels and small sharks, and squids. The coelacanth is a drift-hunter that glides with the current and pounces on its prey. They may find their prey by detecting the electrical signals that the prey send out. Coelacanths hunt mainly at night and shelter from their predators in caves during the day. Coelacanths are preyed on by giant sharks.

How are coelacanths caught?

All the coelacanths caught in the Comoros have been hooked on long fishing lines by local fishermen in dugout canoes or galawas who were trying to catch oilfish. Oilfish are large fish that live at the same depth as coelacanths and are valued for their flesh and oils. Coelacanths are not good to eat. Between one and 11 coelacanths are caught each year by fishermen, who go out mainly at night. The coelacanth, called 'gombessa' in the Comoros, had little value before Western scientists showed an interest in it. Conservationists are trying to lessen the fishing pressure on the coelacanth.

COELACANTH FISHERMAN

Where was the first coelacanth caught?

The first coelacanth known to scientists was caught in December 1938 in a trawl net off the Chalumna River. The second coelacanth was hooked off Anjouan island in the Comoros in 1952 and the third off Grand Comoro in 1953. Comoran fishermen have probably been catching coelacanths for centuries as over 180 of these fish have been caught off the Comoros since 1938. In August 1991 a coelacanth was caught off Mozambique near Quelimane, which tells us that coelacanths may live off the African coast.

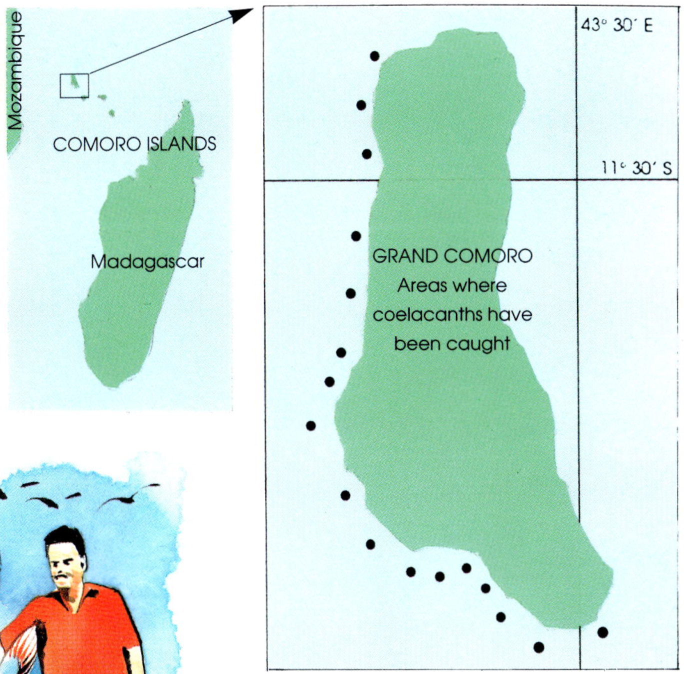

How big does a coelacanth grow?

The largest coelacanth ever recorded was about the size of a big man – 178 centimetres long and weighing 98 kilograms. This large specimen was caught off the coast of Mozambique in 1991. Another coelacanth which was caught off Grand Comoro in 1960 measured 180 centimetres and weighed 95 kilograms. Male coelacanths are smaller than the females and all the very large specimens are females. We know from the fossil record that most extinct coelacanths were small.

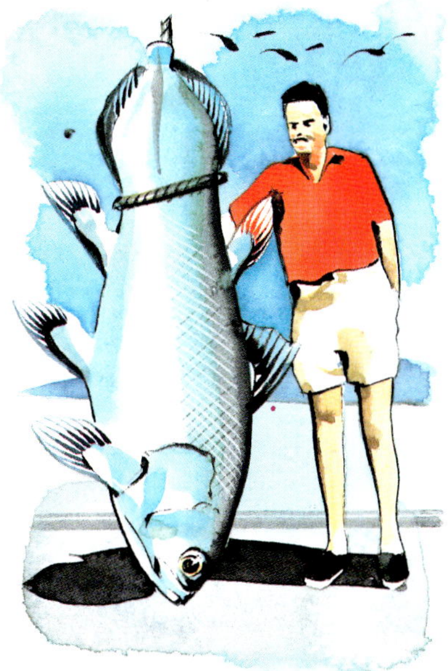

How do coelacanths breed?

Coelacanths do not lay eggs but give birth to live young. The developing pups absorb yolk from their large yolksacs. Oxygen and food may also pass directly from the mother to the young. The young fish are quite large at birth and as many as 26 may be born at a time!

Is the coelacanth threatened with extinction?

Yes. Their numbers are very low and they only live off a few islands in the western Indian Ocean and maybe on the African coast. If we catch too many the one remaining coelacanth species may also disappear forever. Coelacanths could also die out if we catch too many of their prey or pollute their deep water habitat. The coelacanth is one of the most beautiful and interesting fishes in the sea and it is important that we conserve it.

JUVENILE COELACANTH

THREATENED COELACANTH

Modern bony fishes

Bony fishes make up about 90 per cent of all living fishes and are the most common of all backboned animals. They typically have jaws, a bony skeleton, paired fins and two pairs of nostrils. There are three main groups of bony fishes: lungfishes, coelacanths and rayfinned fishes. The bony fishes first evolved about 500 million years ago and have diversified into a bewildering array of forms. Many fishes that are familiar to us, such as sardines, trouts, eels, kobs, marlins, gobies and most tropical reef fishes, are bony fishes.

Which is the deadliest fish?

Probably the stonefish, which is well camouflaged and has several dorsal spines with sacs of neurotoxic venom at their bases. An unwary wader or swimmer who stands on the spines may be injected with poison, which is very painful and often fatal. The stonefish is found in the Red Sea and in tropical parts of the Pacific and Indian Oceans as far south as Durban. The lionfish and eel-catfish are less dangerous fishes but we still have to be careful when we handle them as they have poison in their fin spines.

What is countershading?

Fishes living in the well-lit open waters of the sea, such as kingfishes and needlefishes, are countershaded to disguise their shape and to blend in with the featureless background light of the sea. When they are looked at from above, their dark backs match the colour of the deep ocean. Seen from below, they look like silvery streaks against a mirror.

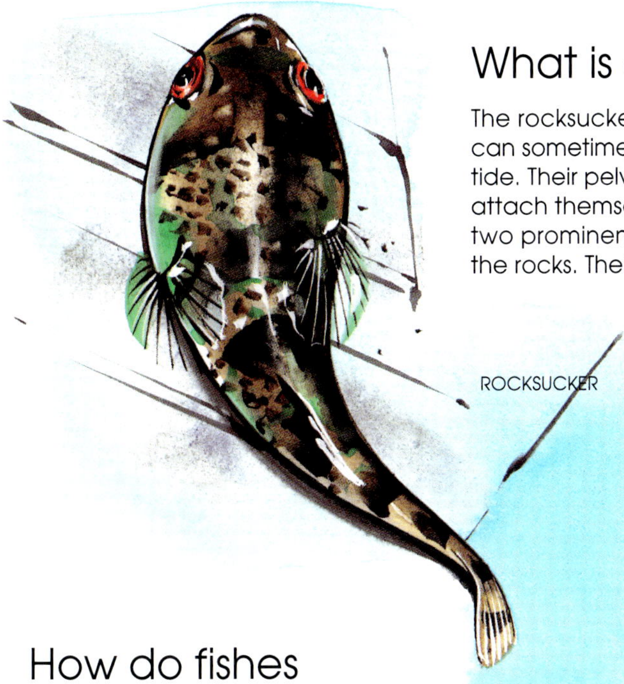

ROCKSUCKER

What is a rocksucker?

The rocksucker is a kind of giant clingfish that lives close to the shore and can sometimes be found attached to rocks in crevices above water at low tide. Their pelvic fins are formed into a large sucking disc which they use to attach themselves to rocks so that they are not washed away. They have two prominent teeth which are used to lever sea urchins and limpets off the rocks. Their dried-up carcasses are sometimes found on the beach.

How do fishes produce their silvery colour?

The silvery, shiny colours of fishes, such as sardines, are produced in special cells in the skin. These cells, called iridocytes, contain crystals of guanin arranged in layers which reflect the different colours of light. Guanin taken from fishes is used to make silver paint.

How do fishes change colour?

The non-shiny colours of fishes are produced in pigment cells called chromatophores. Each cell contains a different colour pigment (yellow, red, orange, black, etc). The pigment granules can be moved around in the cell. When the pigment is spread throughout the cell the colour is brighter, but when the granules are concentrated the brightness is lessened. The contraction and expansion of the pigments brings about the changes in colour pattern, for example, when a Cape stumpnose changes from a silvery colour to silver with dark crossbars at night.

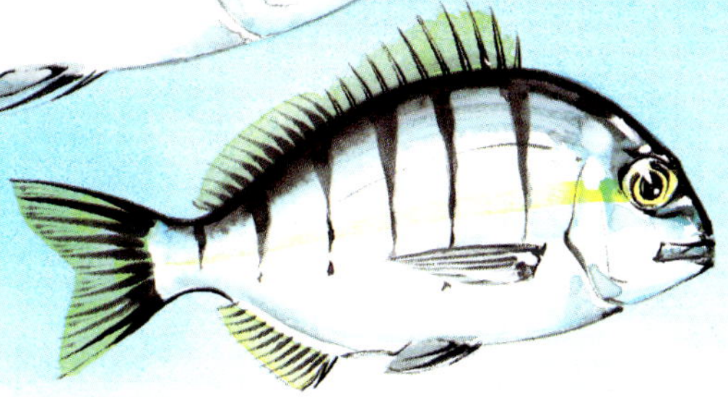

CAPE STUMPNOSE

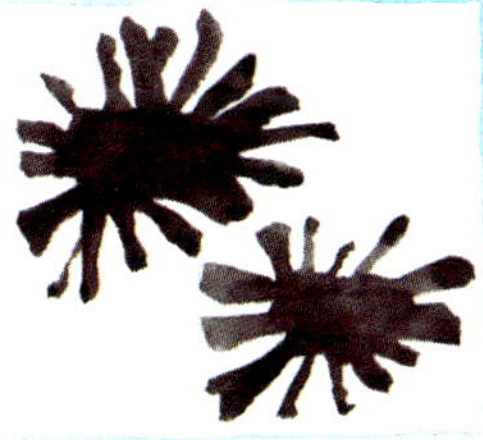

CHROMATOPHORES

LEFTEYE FLOUNDER

Why do fishes change colour?

To match different backgrounds and to send messages to other fishes. A galjoen, for example, is dark when it swims among rocks but changes to a paler colour when it swims over sand. Soles and flounders have an amazing ability to change colour so that they are camouflaged against different colour backgrounds. When fishes are breeding or fighting they may have brighter colours. Fishes often have different colour patterns during the day and at night, and may show the night pattern if they are frightened during the day. Young fishes, such as the African coris, have completely different colours from the adults.

Fish shapes and structures

We usually think of fishes as silver, slippery, streamlined animals but most are quite different from this description. Many fishes have long bodies whereas others are short and deep. Some are round whereas others are flattened. The fins may form complicated shapes or may not even be present at all. Fishes have probably adopted a greater variety of shapes and sizes than any other group of backboned animals.

Can fishes breathe air?

Most fishes remove oxygen from the water using their gills, but some are able to breathe air. The ability to breathe air is highly developed in some freshwater fishes. The lungfishes, for example, have both gills and lungs. Some marine fishes are also able to breathe air. The mudhopper, which waddles around on mudflats in mangrove swamps, breathes through its skin. Mullet that are trapped in warm, stagnant water often jump out of the water to take in air which is then kept in bubbles in a chamber above the gills.

Why do fish have swimbladders?

Swimbladders help fishes to float in midwater. Gas is pumped in or out to change the buoyancy. If a fish is pulled too quickly to the surface, the gas in the bladder cannot adjust quickly enough to the decreasing pressure. The bladder then either bursts or pushes the internal organs out through the mouth. Some fishes have lost their swimbladders or they have become filled with fat. The bladders of coelacanths are filled with lipids or low density oils.

What is the lateral line?

The lateral line is a sense organ that runs along the head and body of a fish and is used to pick up low frequency sound or other vibrations in the water. The kob has a lateral line that is easy to see. The small sensory organs or hair cells in the lateral line are sensitive to the vibrations that are caused by fishes swimming nearby. By listening to one another using their lateral line organs, shoaling fishes such as anchovies are able to swim in tight formation and avoid bumping into each other in a school.

How do fishes produce sounds?

The swimbladder is used by some fishes to make or amplify sounds. Muscles which are attached to the gas-filled swimbladder are contracted to produce sound waves that are heard as growls, yelps, whistles, grunts, hoots and drumming noises. These noises are either used to chase away predators or to attract mates. Grunters and kobs are well known fishes that produce sounds. Male rat-tails use special muscles to make a drumming sound on their swimbladder to attract the female. Once you have learned how to listen underwater, you will find that the sea is not a silent world at all!

Can marine fishes live in fresh water?

Some sea fishes, such as bull sharks, sawfishes, glassies, silversides, sleepers, gobies, moonies, mullets and kobs are able to survive in estuaries and rivers. This is because these fishes can tolerate wide changes in salt concentrations, or salinity, from 35 parts per thousand (sea water) to 0 parts per thousand (fresh water). The Mozambique tilapia, which is normally a freshwater fish, is so tolerant of sea water that it has even been found breeding in the sea. Zambezi sharks and sawfishes have been caught in rivers hundreds of kilometres upstream of the estuary.

Why doesn't the blood of Antarctic fishes freeze?

Some, like the bullhead notothen, have 'anti-freeze' chemicals in their blood which stop them from freezing in the -1 degree to -2 degrees Celsius water temperatures in which they live. The freezing point of fish blood is -1,2 degrees Celsius but the anti-freezes lower the freezing point to -2,2 degrees Celsius. Anti-freezes are found in about 15 species of notothens in the Southern Ocean.

Did you know?

Scientists have found that the slightly rough skin of a shark allows water to flow over it more smoothly than over a completely smooth skin. Modern aircraft wings and bodies have now been designed with the same slightly rough surface so that they can fly more smoothly through the air.

BULLHEAD NOTOTHEN

Senses of fishes

The sense organs of fishes pick up physical or chemical signals in the water. Changes in water temperature or touch are felt through skin receptors. Light signals are received through the eyes, and sounds or vibrations are picked up through the inner ear or lateral line. Chemical stimuli are picked up by the smell or taste organs.

Do fishes feel pain?

When a Roman is caught on a hook and line, it can definitely feel through its nervous system that it has been hooked, and will try to escape. Unlike humans, most fishes have no frontal lobe in their primitive brains and so they are not likely to be distressed by any pain that they feel. It is nevertheless cruel to cut open or otherwise damage a fish that is still alive.

Can fishes smell?

Yes, a goatfish can smell even the smallest traces of chemicals in the water or in the sand using its sense cells. The sense of smell is used to trace prey, to find mates, to avoid danger and to find familiar places. Sharks and rays have a very good sense of smell. Some fishes, such as sea catfish, rely more on smell than sight to find their prey. Mullet use their sense of smell to find their way from the sea to estuaries.

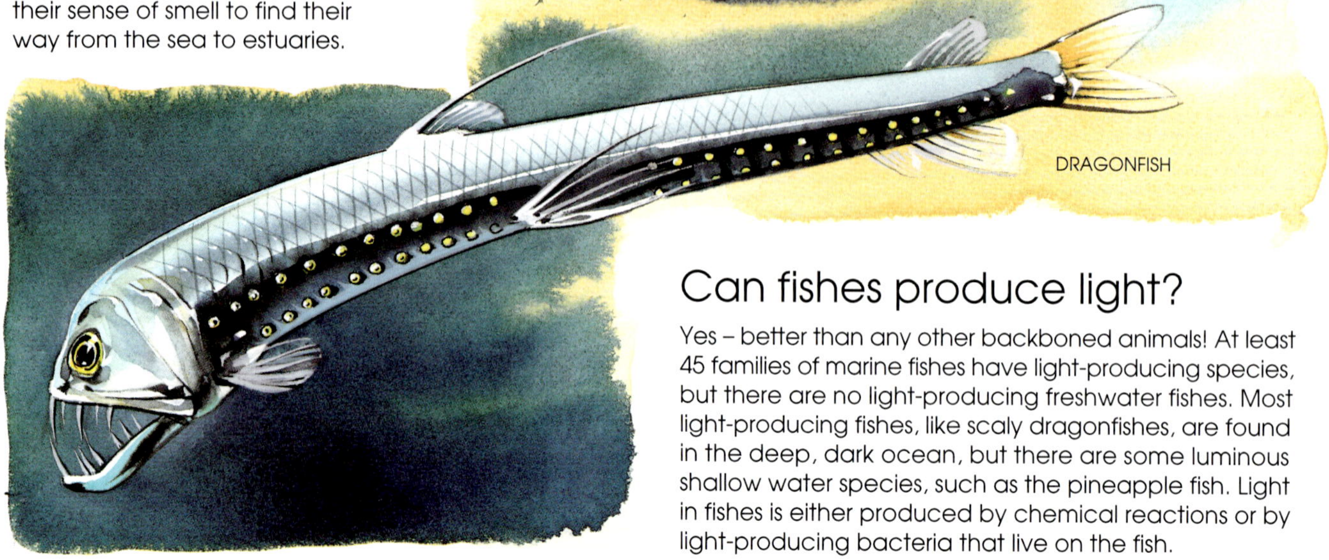

Can fishes produce light?

Yes – better than any other backboned animals! At least 45 families of marine fishes have light-producing species, but there are no light-producing freshwater fishes. Most light-producing fishes, like scaly dragonfishes, are found in the deep, dark ocean, but there are some luminous shallow water species, such as the pineapple fish. Light in fishes is either produced by chemical reactions or by light-producing bacteria that live on the fish.

ANGLERFISH

Why do fishes produce light?

Deepsea anglerfish have light organs suspended on long tendrils which they dangle in the water to attract unsuspecting prey. The scaleless dragonfishes, for example, find their prey using headlights that produce a red light which their prey cannot see. The viperfish has lights inside its mouth to attract prey. Dim lights on the body of a fish camouflage it as they break up its outline. Many fishes have patterns of lights on their bodies that are different from those of other fishes so that their mates can recognise them.

Which fish uses a flashlight?

The flashlight fish has a large light-producing organ under the eye where there is a colony of millions of bacteria. The light organ is switched off by turning it downwards into a black pocket under the eye. The lights are used to confuse predators. When it sees an attacker the flashlight fish swims in a straight line then suddenly closes off its light, changes direction and rushes away.

FLASHLIGHT FISH

Can fish see colour?

Yes, many species of shallow water fishes, such as parrotfishes, wrasses, angelfishes and butterflyfishes, can see different colours. Fishes that live in well-lit, shallow waters, like the longnose butterflyfish, have mainly cone cells in the retina of their eyes so that they can clearly see colours. Deepsea fishes, like eelpouts, have mainly rod cells in their retinas so that they can see at low light levels. Many deepsea fishes are colour blind. In the deepest parts of the oceans fishes have tiny eyes or are completely blind.

LONGNOSE BUTTERFLYFISH

EEL-CATFISH

Can fishes stun their prey?

The marbled electric ray uses strong electrical discharges made in special kidney-shaped organs on each side of the body to stun its prey. Anglers, divers and swimmers receive a nasty shock if they stand on these fishes! Torpedo rays can give off a 220-volt shock and electric catfishes in fresh water can give off an even more deadly 300-volt shock.

Do fishes really detect electrical signals?

Sharks, rays and many bony fishes, such as the eel-catfish, have electrical sense organs that can detect the electrical fields of other animals. Sharks and rays living on the sea bottom have many electrical sense organs in their heads and find prey buried in the sand or at night using these electroreceptors. Some fishes may even use their electric organs to navigate during long journeys through the ocean by following the magnetic field of the Earth.

MARBLED ELECTRIC RAY

Where fishes live

Water is everything to fishes. It is their freeway, nursery, school, playground, house, toilet and grave. Fishes live in the deepest parts of the oceans and in cold lakes on top of mountains. Fishes can also be found in freshwater lakes and in lagoons where the salt content is three times higher than sea water. From this we can see that fishes thrive in the cold Arctic and Antarctic as well as in hot tropical lakes and rivers. They also live in underground waters and cave lakes.

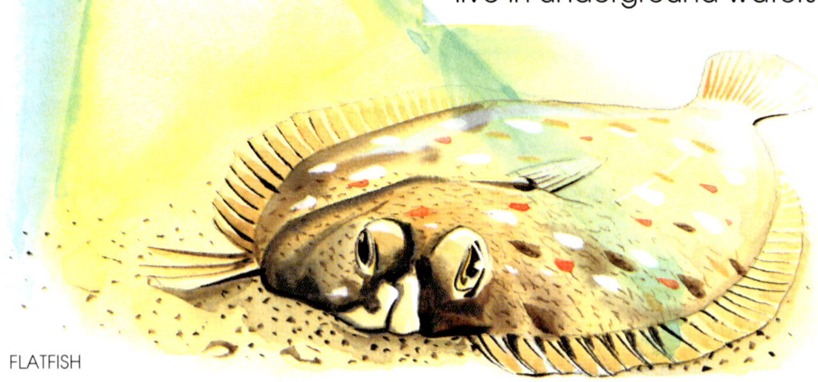

FLATFISH

How deep do fishes live?

Fishes have been seen from research submarines in the deepest parts of the oceans. A flatfish was found at a depth of 10 911 metres near the bottom of the Mariana Trench in the Pacific Ocean. The average depth of the oceans is over 1 500 metres and most fish like to live in the shallower half where there is more food.

Why is the pearlfish not a welcome guest?

They live inside a sea cucumber! The sea cucumber tries to stop the pearlfish from entering its body, but when it opens its breathing hole, the pearlfish slips in tail first and rests with its head poking out. The pearlfish sometimes eats parts of the internal organs of the sea cucumber, so it is not very welcome.

PEARLFISH IN A SEA CUCUMBER

Are sharks really the monsters of the deep?

No, not all are. In fact, most sharks, such as dogfishes and rays, live in shallow water around the edge of the ocean but some live in the surf zone, or in water deeper than 3 000 metres. Sharks can be found in the tropics and, less commonly, in cool and cold oceans. Some sharks are active by day, and others by night. Some live by themselves whereas others live in groups.

DOGFISH

RAY

Are there any sessile fishes?

Yes, garden eels are sessile fishes because they stay in one place throughout their adult lives. They live tail-down in a hole in the sand in colonies or groups. Garden eels sway gently to and fro in the current while they wait for small prey to drift past them. When they are frightened, they slip backwards into their burrows.

Can fishes live in hot springs?

Yes. Some freshwater fishes that live in hot springs feel comfortable in temperatures which reach higher than 40 degrees Celsius! This is even hotter than a hot bath! Fishes in the Antarctic and Arctic live at near freezing temperatures, but most fishes live in water that is warmer than10 degrees and cooler than 30 degrees Celsius.

Why do some fishes live with shrimps?

The pinkbar goby, like many other gobies, lives in a burrow with a shrimp so that it can share housekeeping duties. The goby digs the burrow and catches prey. The shrimp eats the scraps of left-over food and cleans out the burrow. Both the shrimp and the goby keep a lookout for predators.

Did you know?

African mudhoppers are fishes that spend most of their lives out of water! They live in muddy mangrove swamps and waddle around on the mud looking for small crabs and worms to eat. Mudhoppers are able to stay out of water for long periods as they can breathe air through their skin and modified gills. They can also take up oxygen through their tails and you will notice, if you observe them carefully, that they sometimes let their tails dangle in a pool of water so that they can breathe through them!

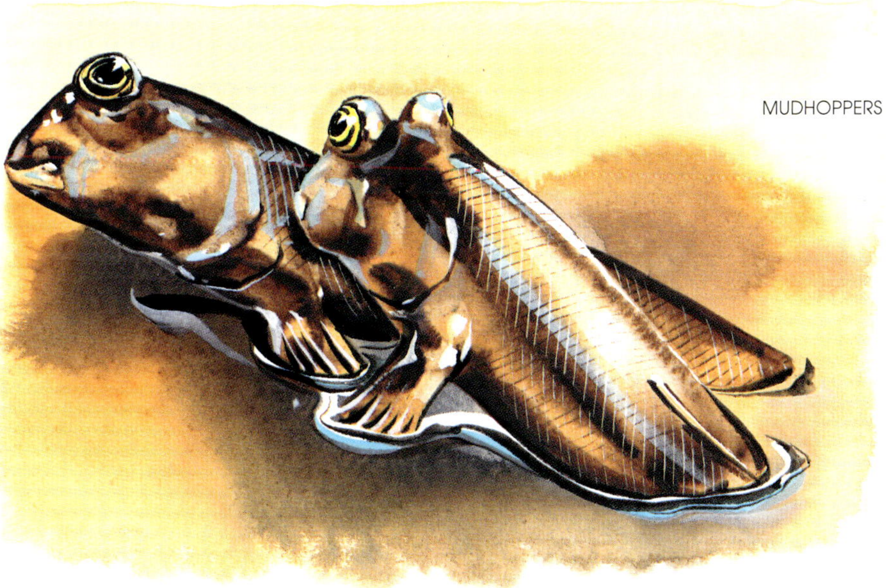

Raising a family

Most fishes hatch from small eggs. These eggs are scattered in open water and are not protected by the parents. Some fishes lay eggs in nests or crevices where they are guarded by their parents. A smaller group of advanced fishes are bearers. This means that their eggs hatch inside the mother's body. When the small juvenile fishes are born, they look like the adults. Fishes which do not guard their young usually lay large numbers of small eggs but guarders and bearers lay fewer, larger eggs and give birth to large young.

OCEAN SUNFISH

Which fish produces millions of eggs?

The ocean sunfish lays over 30 million small eggs each time it breeds! The reason why this fish can lay so many eggs is because of its huge size. It is over three metres long and weighs about 2 800 kilograms. They swim in the open ocean, often near the surface, and feed on jellyfish and large zooplankton. Baby sunfishes look very different from the adults and were once thought to be a different species.

Which fish lays the least eggs?

The fewest eggs are produced by a mouthbrooding fish from Lake Tanganyika which lays seven or less eggs each time it breeds. A pregnant coelacanth caught in the Comoros in 1962 contained only five developing young but other coelacanths have had as many as 26 fertilised eggs. The egg of the coelacanth is about the size of an orange and is the largest egg of any fish.

Where do freshwater eels breed?

In the open sea. When the large eels that live in our rivers are ready to breed, they swim down to the sea and then carry out a remarkable journey all the way to the western Indian Ocean where they breed. The larval eels, called leptocephali, drift southwards with the currents and change into tiny, transparent glass eels which enter our rivers during summer. Once in the river, the glass eel becomes coloured and, as an elver, swims to the top of the river, where it lives for 10 to 15 years.

FRESHWATER EELS

Do manta rays give birth by jumping out of the water?

Probably. It is known that manta rays give birth to live young. At least two people, one in South Africa and one in California, have seen giant manta rays jump out of the water and fling their newly-born young into the air. Their normal method of giving birth is probably in the water. If you see a manta ray jump out of the water, keep a careful watch for any young that might be born!

Why do some fishes change sex?

A sex change helps a fish produce more young. If it is one sex (for example, a female) when it is small and changes into the other sex (male) when it is large, then it can mate with the other females and have more young. Many species of marine fishes change sex during their life cycles. About 20 of the 40 species of seabreams in southern Africa change sex, either from males to females or from females to males. The Roman, a common angling species, changes from a female that lives in groups to a male that lives by itself during its life cycle.

Do male seahorses give birth?

No, but it does seem as if he does because the female places her eggs in a pouch on the male's body. It is then the male seahorse's job to protect the developing eggs and juveniles in the pouch until they are large enough to fend for themselves. There are six species of seahorses in southern Africa. The Knysna seahorse, which lives in lagoons and estuaries along the southern Cape coast, may die out if we do not take better care of its environment.

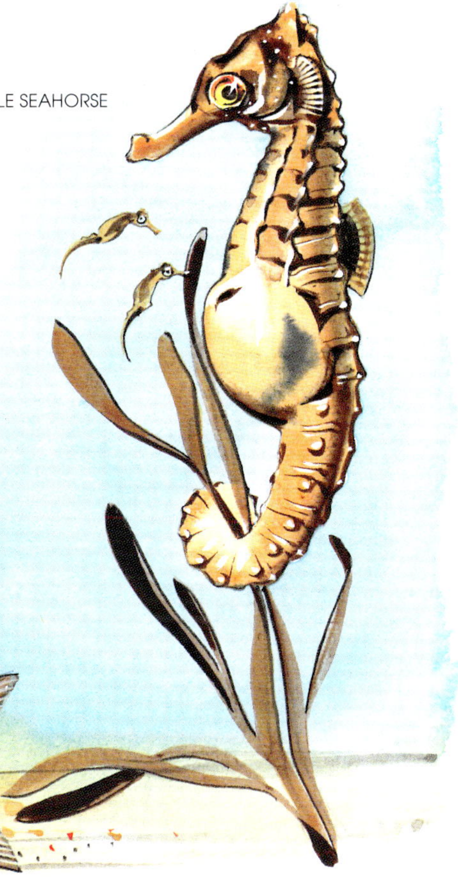

How do sea catfish care for their young?

The males care for the eggs and young in their mouths. The eggs are the size of small marbles and hatch in the mouth. The young fishes swim out of their father's mouth to feed but scurry back when danger threatens. Cardinal fishes also care for their eggs and young in their mouths.

Feeding and growing

Fishes, like all animals, need food in order to survive and grow. Some fishes feed entirely on plants and others feed only on animals, including other fishes. Some fishes feed on both plants and animals. Many fishes filter out plankton, the microscopic plants and animals that float in the sea, and others feed on micro-organisms in the bottom mud. Worms, coral polyps, snails, crabs and shrimps are important food items for fishes.

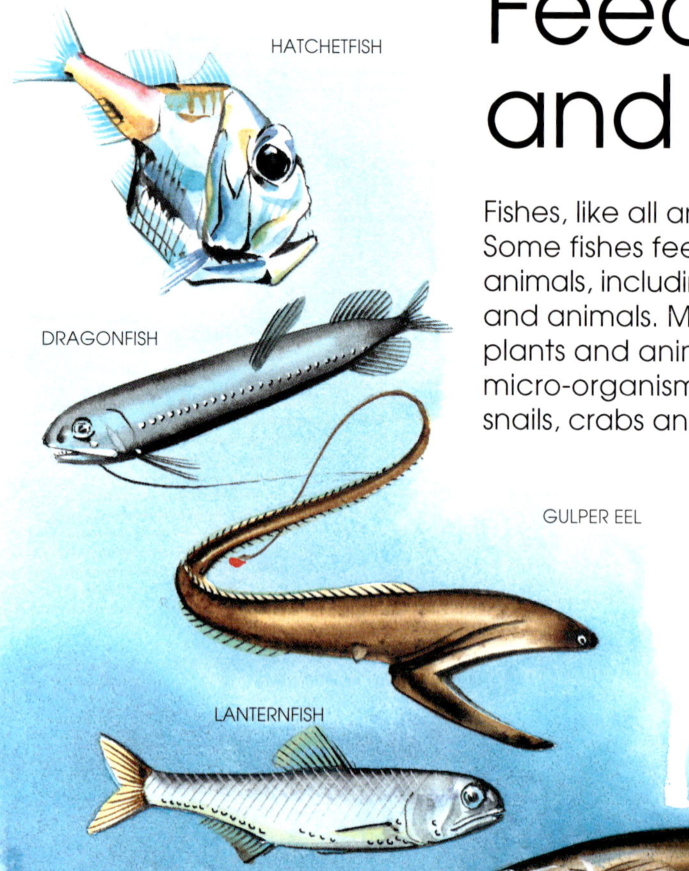

What do deepsea fishes eat?

Some deepsea fishes, such as the eelpouts, feed on snails, crabs and bristleworms which themselves feed in the bottom mud on the remains of plants and animals that drift down into the depths from the well-lit surface layers. Other deepsea fishes are ambush predators which creep up on other fishes in the dark and attack. As the deep ocean is permanently dark, many deepsea fishes are blind.

How does the gulper eel feed?

Because food is hard to find in the dark depths, each meal has to last a long time. Gulper eels have enormous mouths for swallowing fishes as large as themselves. They swim slowly with their jaws stretched wide open in order to catch prey. There is a light on the tip of the tail which attracts the prey closer.

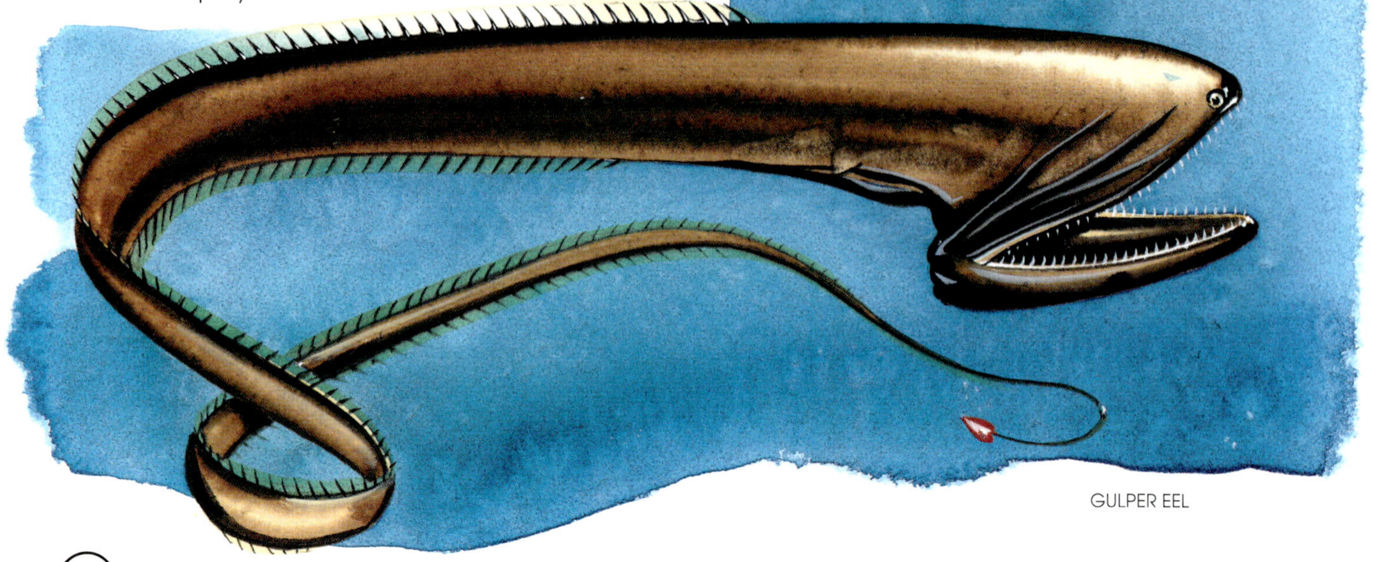

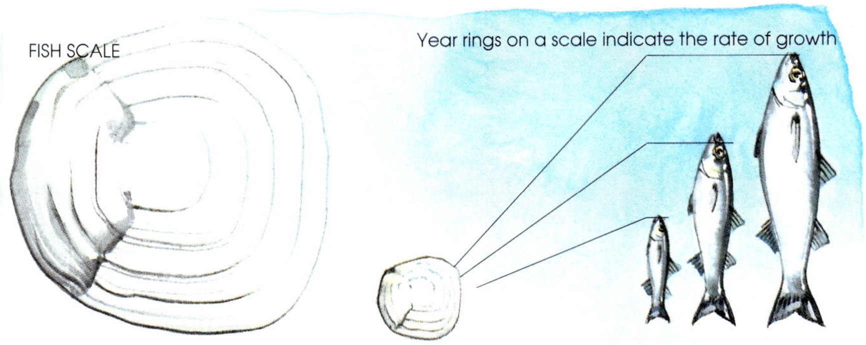

How do you tell the age of a fish?

By counting the rings on its scales, otoliths (ear bones) or fin spines. Many fishes lay down one ring each year but some lay down more than one ring each year, so working out the age is not always easy! In some fishes daily growth rings are laid down on the ear bones. Once we know the age of a fish we are also able to say how quickly it grows and how old it gets.

How long do fishes live?

Larger fishes usually live longer than smaller ones. Very small gobies may only live for one or two years. Most marine fishes live for three to eight years but large sharks, groupers and rockcods can live longer than 25 years! Tunas and billfishes grow very quickly and probably do not live longer than 15 years. The coelacanth grows slowly and can probably live as long as 60 years.

AGES OF FISHES

Do fishes grow all the time?

Yes, fishes grow all their lives but they grow slower as they become older. The kob grows at a rate of 15 to 20 centimetres each year while it is young and reaches a length of 75 centimetres after four years. Later in life they grow at less than 10 centimetres a year. When they are 16 years old they are about 150 centimetres long.

The arms race

One of the laws of the sea is eat or be eaten! Predators are constantly chasing prey and prey are always on the lookout for the predator. Predators make use of speed and stealth, camouflage and pack hunting as well as large teeth and a wide gape as a way of catching a meal! Prey find ways of protecting themselves and so make it harder to be caught. They rely on speed and camouflage, as well as hiding and shoaling behaviour to stay alive. Prey may also be protected by bizarre spines, armour plating and poisons in the never-ending battle with their enemies.

HUMPBACK WHALE

Which marine animal catches fishes with a bubble net?

The humpback whale. The whale swims in a circle underneath a shoal of fishes, letting out a stream of bubbles from its blowhole. The fishes are surrounded by a 'net' of glistening bubbles and, although they could swim through it, they become confused and remain inside the 'net' where they are caught by the whale.

Can fish change colour?

Yes. Many fishes are masters of camouflage and can change their colour, like a chameleon, so that they match their background. At night, the fusilier fish sleeps near the sea bed and is darkly coloured to match its background. During the day it swims up into the bright surface waters to feed and changes to a pale, translucent colour.

FUSILIER FISH

Why does the porcupinefish blow itself up?

When a porcupinefish is surprised by a predator it swallows water and blows itself up to the size of a small football. The spines on the body stick out and most attackers are either scared off or are unable to swallow their prey. Dried, blown-up porcupinefishes are used as lampshades and ornaments.

PORCUPINEFISH

Are any fishes poisonous?

Yes, there are several poisonous fishes. The liver, reproductive organs, muscles and intestine of puffers are very poisonous and other fish will not eat them. In Japan, people eat the puffer, which is regarded as a delicacy, but an expert chef must first remove the poisonous organs and make the flesh safe. Still, the puffer or fugu continues to kill people every year in Japan. The liver of the red steenbras, and probably of tunas and some sharks, shouldn't be eaten because, like the livers of the seal and the polar bear, they have a very high vitamin A content. Eating their livers may result in nausea and stomach cramps.

Why are some fish brightly coloured?

Puffer fishes are brightly coloured to warn predators that they are poisonous or not very tasty. Butterflyfishes use their bright colours to attract mates. In some fishes, bright colours are used to show aggression or submission or to frighten off rivals for mates or territories. Many fishes have five or more colour patterns to suit their different moods.

Can fishes really fly?

Flyingfishes swim near the water surface. When a predator attacks they project themselves out of the water at speed and spread their broad fins out to glide rather than fly. They take off at about 64 kilometres per hour and can glide for over 1 000 metres. They confuse most of their predators by gliding through the air but dolphinfish are able to follow their flight paths and catch the flyingfish as they flop back into the water.

FLYINGFISH

Did you know?

There are several kinds of fishes in South Africa with poisonous spines, including stingrays, catfishes, rabbitfishes, scorpionfishes, stonefishes, turkeyfishes and firefishes. Turkeyfishes, though small and slow-moving, can be quite aggressive and have been known to attack a swimmer. They occur along the east and south coast – admire them but beware!

Peculiar behaviour

People have been interested in how fishes behave ever since they started to catch them for food. Feeding and breeding are the most important behaviour of fishes. Feeding is essential for the survival of individual fishes and breeding enables the fish to have offspring, making sure that the species survives. Other behaviour, such as avoiding predators, help the fish to remain healthy and safe when it is not feeding and breeding.

Why do fishes migrate?

Migrations are regular mass movements of fishes from one place to another, usually to feed or breed. These migrations take place along the coast or from deep to shallow water. The elf migrates from KwaZulu-Natal to the southern Cape coast in late summer and returns to KwaZulu-Natal in spring. Lanternfishes migrate several hundred metres upwards into shallow water each evening to feed on the plankton.

What is the sardine run?

Sardines or pilchards are cool water fishes that normally live off the southern and western Cape. During winter, a band of cool water forms along the coasts of the eastern Cape and KwaZulu-Natal and the sardines, together with anchovies and round herrings, migrate northwards, perhaps to find new feeding grounds. They are sometimes washed onto the beaches in large numbers and are caught by local people.

Shark

Do fishes hitchhike?

Yes. The remora is a hitchhiking scavenger that attaches itself by a sucker to large fish, such as sharks or manta rays, as well as to dolphins, turtles and even ships! When its host finds food, the remora lets go and feeds on the scraps. The remora attaches itself using a vacuum sucker which has ridges on it to stop it from being detached from its host unless it swims forward. Another hitchhiker is the male anglerfish, which is far smaller than the female and attaches itself to her for life. When she lays her eggs the male is nearby to fertilise them.

What do cleaner fish eat?

They remove parasites and dead skin from large fishes. The cleaners work inside the mouths and gills as well as over the bodies of their 'patients'. Both fishes benefit as the cleaner obtains a free meal and the large fish gets rid of its parasites. The cleaner fish perform peculiar dances that enable the large fish to identify them. Several wrasses are cleaners when they are young but feed on coral polyps as adults. Coral shrimps also act as cleaners, especially for moray eels.

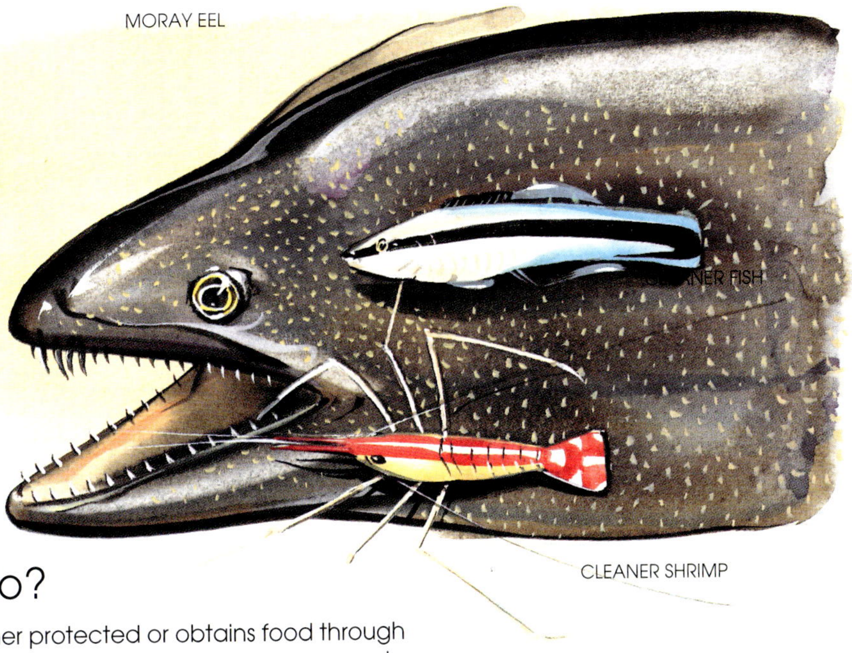

What does a mimic do?

A mimic imitates another fish and is either protected or obtains food through mimicry. The sabre-toothed blenny closely resembles a cleaner wrasse and swims in a similar way. Large fish are fooled by the mimic and allow it to come close. The blenny then takes a small bite of flesh from the unsuspecting fish. Some wrasses are fish-eating predators that change colour and mimic harmless plant-eating fishes. They approach prey by swimming in a shoal of harmless fishes until they are close enough to dart out and catch their prey.

Why is the clownfish safe from the tentacles of an anemone?

A special secretion protects the clownfish from the stings of the sea anemone. The clownfish lives among the anemone's tentacles, where it is safe from predators. In return, the clownfish attracts other fish which dart into the tentacles where they are caught by the anemone. This is a good example of symbiosis, which means living together so that both partners benefit.

Do fishes sleep?

Yes, they do but without closing their eyes! Many fishes rest on the bottom or in caves and crevices at night, depending on whether they have fed during the day. Others sleep during the day but hunt at night. The parrotfish forms an amazing mucous envelope around it when it sleeps. Many wrasses bury themselves in the sand at night to sleep.

Conservation of fishes

KNYSNA SEAHORSE

Large numbers of plants and animals live along the shallow edge of the sea. The open ocean, in contrast, doesn't have much life, so it is rather like a semi-desert and the deep ocean is like a desert. Fishes were once thought to exist in huge numbers but we know now that they can easily be overfished by Man. Because we live on land we have been less concerned about conservation in the water. It is also difficult to study life under water and we are not sure how many fishes are threatened or endangered by our activities.

Are there any threatened marine fishes in South Africa?

Yes! There are at least nine marine and estuarine fishes which live in South African waters that are endangered, vulnerable or rare throughout their world range. The coelacanth, great white shark, Knysna seahorse, and bearded eelgoby may become extinct if we do not look after them more carefully. The freshwater mullet, golden sleeper, checked goby, barebreast goby and burrowing goby are very rare and also need protection. Sadly, the river pipefish has recently become extinct in South Africa.

What threatens our fish populations?

Overfishing, pollution, interference with ecological processes and changes to their habitat are the main reasons why fishes have become scarcer. Many people don't seem to care. Anglers, aquarists, commercial fishermen, divers and holidaymakers all need to work together to conserve fishes. You can help too! Learn as much as you can about fishes from books and field observations, then share your knowledge and fascination with others. Also learn about the rules of angling, bait collection and using a beach, and stay within the law. Visit oceanaria and museums to learn about fishes. Support conservation groups that campaign against pollution, environmental disturbance and overfishing.

DIVER WITH FISH

FISH BEING RELEASED

How can anglers conserve fish?

Many anglers are strong supporters of conservation. They catch only as many fish as they need, and tag and release some of their catch. They co-operate in the fish research programmes of local museums, research institutes and universities. They are aware that lead sinkers, which are often lost while fishing, may pollute the water. They use a new biodegradable sinker that decomposes into fish food after five months underwater. Other anglers use small bags of sand as sinkers. Many anglers avoid using stainless steel hooks as they do not rust quickly underwater like ordinary hooks. Hooks that do not rust are a constant threat to underwater life. Anglers who care about the environment do not throw plastic or oil into the water.

What is an alien fish?

A fish that has been introduced by Man into areas beyond its natural range. Alien fishes may damage natural communities by feeding on local fishes, introducing parasites and diseases, breeding with local fishes, disturbing the habitat and interfering with the territories of local fishes. As far as possible, communities of fishes and other animals that evolved together should not be disrupted by the introduction of alien species. Don't release your aquarium fish into the wild – it is illegal!

ALIEN CRAB

Did you know?

The Tsitsikamma National Park on the southern Cape coast is the oldest marine reserve in Africa. The Park was established in 1964 and stretches for 72 kilometres along the coast and for five kilometres out to sea. Many important angling fishes and shellfishes feed and breed in the Park. Some of these fishes then swim into overfished areas on either side of the Park and so restock these waters.

Are there any alien marine fishes in southern Africa?

Not yet, as far as we know, but they are likely to be introduced if we are not careful. There are alien fishes on the east and west coasts of North America as well as in Europe and Japan. Many of these fishes were introduced in the water that ships carry to weigh them down when they have no cargo (ballast water). Alien crabs, mussels and snails have been introduced into South Africa and have caused considerable disruptions to natural marine communities.

Could I find a new species of fish?

Yes. Many new species of fishes have been found by children, holidaymakers or anglers who knew enough about fishes to recognise that their specimen was different, and took it to a local scientist to be identified. If you find a new species of fish it may even be named after you! Whenever you are at the beach you have a chance of discovering something new.

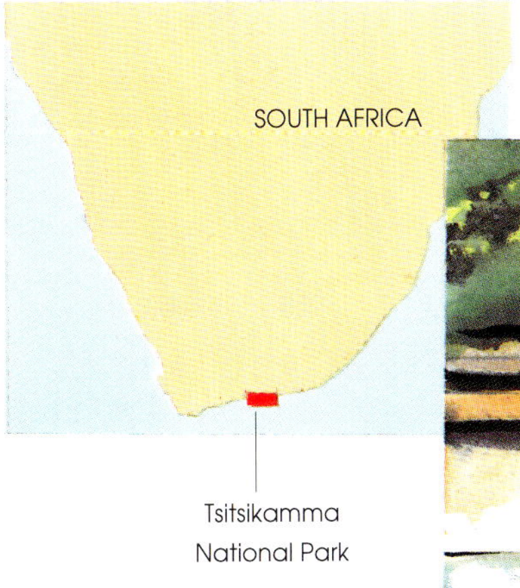

Uses of fishes

Fishes are used by people in more different ways than any other animals. They are caught for food or fun and are used to make stock feed, fertilisers, glues, paints, oils and medicines. They are also kept in aquaria and ponds for decoration, used for the biological control of pests, and make useful subjects for scientific study. The beautiful shapes and colours of fishes are a source of inspiration to artists and craftsmen. Fishes are also vitally important as links in the food chain, especially as predators and prey in the sea and fresh water.

TRADITIONAL FISHING

How were fishes first caught in southern Africa?

Fishes were an important part of the diet of the early people of southern Africa who lived near the coast. They caught fishes using spears, reed traps, bone hooks, and poisons found in nature. Walls of rocks were made in rocky pools by early Strandlopers to trap fish at low tide. The fish traps at Kosi Bay in Zululand have valves made out of reeds and sticks which allow the fishes to swim in but stop them from escaping. These traps are good examples of traditional fishing methods used by early South Africans. Gillnets made from natural plant fibres and bone hooks are still used by fishermen along the Mozambique coast.

What are unusual uses of fishes?

Dried boxfish have been used as children's rattles, and eel, shark and catfish leather are used to make wallets and shoes. Fish teeth, spines and bones have been used to make daggers, swords, needles and the points of arrows and spears. The dried bodies of porcupinefish make strong war helmets and the backbones of sharks have been used as walking sticks!

PRODUCTS OF FISH LEATHER

HOME AQUARIUM

Are marine fishes good aquarium pets?

Yes, as long as you are prepared to keep their sea water in good condition. A properly maintained marine aquarium is a beautiful, living work of art in a home or classroom. Butterflyfishes, damselfishes, surgeonfishes, triggerfishes, squirrelfishes and cardinal fishes are the most popular marine aquarium fishes.